D1708197

EXPERIENCE NATURE

How Time Outside Makes You Feel

by Jean C. Lawler

RED CHAIR •PRESS•

Experience Personal Power books are produced and published by Red Chair Press

Red Chair Press LLC   PO Box 333   South Egremont, MA 01258-0333

www.redchairpress.com

FREE Lesson Plans from Lerner eSource and at www.redchairpress.com

Publisher's Cataloging-In-Publication Data

Names: Lawler, Jean C.

Title: Experience nature : how time outside makes you feel / by Jean C. Lawler.

Other Titles: How time outside makes you feel

Description: South Egremont, Massachusetts : Red Chair Press, [2018] | Series: Experience personal power | Interest age level: 007-010. | Includes bold words in context with a glossary and resources for further reading. | Includes index. | Summary: Children learn that spending time in nature can lower their stress and help them to be more focused in and out of the classroom.

Identifiers: ISBN 9781634403733 (library hardcover) | ISBN 9781634403771 (paperback) | ISBN 9781634403818 (ebook)

Subjects: LCSH: Nature--Psychological aspects--Juvenile literature. | Emotions--Juvenile literature. | Stress management--Juvenile literature. | Attention--Juvenile literature. | CYAC: Nature--Psychological aspects. | Emotions. | Stress management. | Attention.

Classification: LCC BF353.5.N37 L39 2018 (print) | LCC BF353.5.N37 (ebook) | DDC 155.91--dc23

LCCN: 2017948345

Illustrations by Nathan Jarvis

Photo credits: Courtesy of the Author 24; iStock Cover, 1, 3-16, 18, 19, 22; Shutterstock 15 (small photo); Spring Rivers 17, 19, 20

Printed in the United States of America

0518 1P CGBF18

Table of Contents

Getting Started:
Think About You

Which would you rather do: go to the mall, be outside with friends, or watch a movie at home?

How often do you go outside with friends and family?

What's your favorite thing to do outside?

Tune In to Nature

What do you think of when you hear the word *nature*? Perhaps a tree, the snow, or your cat? These are all **natural things**. Nature is about living things like humans, plants, and animals. Non-living things like rocks and rainbows are part of nature, too.

Things in nature can be big and small. They can also be hard and soft. Natural things can be near to you and also far away. Some are loud and some are silent.

You can use all your senses to explore nature. See the birds flying. Hear the dog bark. Feel the hot sun on your face. Smell the flowers. Taste the fresh corn.

Natural things are all around you outside. You can see them on a city street, in the forest, at a farm, and up in the sky. You can see nature while walking, looking out your classroom window, riding a bike, and flying in an airplane.

You can bring some natural things indoors, too. Plants can live on a windowsill. You can keep a colorful rock collection in a box. Fish can live in a tank.

Some things you see and use every day are not natural. People make many of the things you see and use. If it is human-made, it is not part of the natural world. Computers, bikes, and even this book are all human-made things.

Notice how you feel when you **interact** with nature. You might feel small standing near a towering tree. Maybe you feel brave picking up a wiggling worm. If you feel angry or sad about something, going outside can help you feel calm. You may sleep better after playing outside.

Make Sense of Being in Nature

There are so many things you can do in nature! You can play in the park. You can exercise by going for a hike. You can explore a local farm or garden to see what is growing. In nature, you can learn a lot about yourself, the food you eat, and your local community.

Start by being **aware** of where you are outside. Look up and down. Look all around. Pay attention to the sights and sounds nearby. Notice what you feel and smell in your space. Using your senses helps you focus on what's happening around you.

Be still for a moment. Take a deep breath in and out. Notice what you feel and think. Being aware of what's happening inside you is important, too. Nature can help.

When it's peaceful outside, you can hear yourself think. Paying attention to your **inner voice** helps you learn about yourself. You can decide what you like and want to do. You can notice what you are feeling.

Power Point

You increase your personal power by breathing fresh air, moving your body, and being quiet and still for a few minutes each day.

Paying attention to your feelings is a healthy thing to do. Let your inner voice help you **be present** with your feelings. Notice if you are happy, sad, worried, or something else.

You get **personal power** when you pay attention to your inner voice. Personal power helps you feel better about yourself and do better in school. It increases your feel-good energy.

Being outside in nature can help you feel better in your body, too. Going for a walk or run is a healthy thing to do. It's healthier than sitting inside with your video games and snacking a lot. Having a balance of inside and outside activities is good for you.

Next time you are outside in nature, notice what you are thinking and how you feel. Do your thoughts and feelings change when you come inside?

Find a place in nature that you like. It could be in a wide-open field or a cozy corner of your backyard. Maybe you'll choose a swing in the schoolyard or your neighborhood park. Think about why you like it there.

Use Your Senses Notice what you see, hear, smell, and feel. Pick one natural thing nearby. Take a photo or make a sketch. Do the same thing once each month. In a journal, write and draw what changes you notice around you.

See Kids in Action

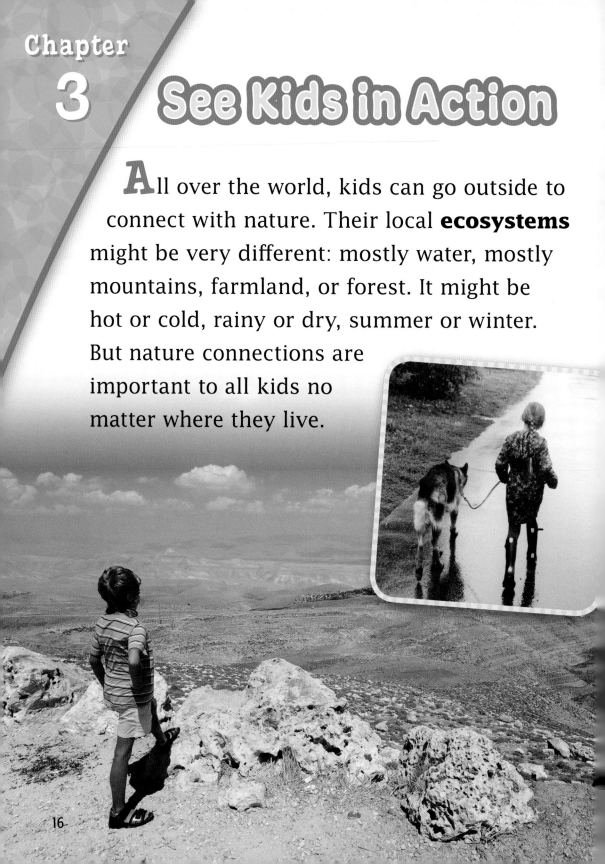

All over the world, kids can go outside to connect with nature. Their local **ecosystems** might be very different: mostly water, mostly mountains, farmland, or forest. It might be hot or cold, rainy or dry, summer or winter. But nature connections are important to all kids no matter where they live.

In California, on the west coast of the United States, the Spring Rivers Outdoor Education Program connects kids with their local ecosystems.

Teachers take kids on hikes along nearby trails. They hunt for "treasures" outside. They explore what they see, hear, feel, and touch. They look for things that are yellow or purple, for example. They listen carefully for sounds that they like. They hunt for something that is prickly. Kids try to find something that smells funny. They experience the wonder of nature all around them.

Writing and drawing are also important parts of the Spring Rivers Program. Kids write poems about what they see, feel, hear, and smell in nature. They write and draw about the sky, the wind, the animals, and the soil.

These California kids spend quiet time outdoors. They take a deep breath in and out and close their eyes. Sitting still, they listen carefully. With eyes open, they notice what they can see, without talking. They pay attention to the feeling of being part of nature. They are gaining personal power.

Moving On:
Taking Action Yourself

Join a nature club at your school or in the community. If there isn't one, get a teacher and some kids together and start one.

Ask a group of friends and family to plan a trip to a park, beach, or campground.

Read books about nature. Learn what nature is like in other parts of the world.

Keep using your journal. Write and draw about what part of being outside you like the most. Learning to know yourself helps build your personal power.

Glossary

aware: knowing that something exists

be present: to notice what is happening right now

ecosystem: living and nonliving things within a certain area

inner voice: thoughts and feelings you have in your own mind/body

interact: to respond to one another

natural things: things not made by humans

personal power: the ability to think and do things that help you succeed

tune in to: to focus on something

For More Information

Books

Cherry, Lynne. *The Great Kapok Tree: A Tale of the Amazon Rain Forest*. Houghton Mifflin Harcourt, 2000

Curtis, Carolyn. *I Took the Moon for a Walk*. Barefoot Books, 2008

Ireland, Karin. *Wonderful Nature, Wonderful You!* Dawn Publications, 2017

Prokos, Anna. *Blades of Green: Adventures in Backyard Habitats*. Red Chair Press, 2017

White, Linda. *Trekking on a Trail: Hiking Adventures for Kids*. Gibbs-Smith, 2000

Magazines to Connect with Nature

National Geographic Kids. Published by the National Geographic Society.

Ranger Rick Junior. Published by the National Wildlife Foundation.

Web Sites

http://www.discovertheforest.org/

http://kids.nationalgeographic.com/

http://www.nhchildreninnature.org/for-kids/links/

http://www.nwf.org/kids/games.aspx

Note to educators and parents: Our editors have carefully reviewed these web sites to ensure they are suitable for children. Web sites change frequently, however, and we cannot guarantee that a site's future contents will continue to meet our high standards of quality and educational value. You may wish to preview these sites and closely supervise children whenever they access the Internet.

Index

About the Author

Jean Lawler loves to be outside! She enjoys the beach, the forest, the farm, and her own backyard. Her favorite thing is to sit outside with a book to read or a journal to write in. She can hear her inner voice and it builds her personal power. Jean says that being in nature, alone and with friends and family, makes her life more *wonder*-ful.